The Unseen Husband

Stephen Disraeli

I would like to dedicate this work to Gillian, friend of Hobbits, who met me as a student atheist and reintroduced me to the Christian faith.

The Unseen Husband

A Survey of the Song of Solomon

Stephen Disraeli

The Unseen Husband by Stephen Disraeli
Copyright © 2022 by Stephen Disraeli
All Rights Reserved.
ISBN: 978-1-59755-674-3
Published by: ADVANTAGE BOOKS™, www.advbookstore.com

This book and parts thereof may not be reproduced in any form, stored in a retrieval system, or transmitted in any form by any means (electronic, mechanical, photocopy, recording or otherwise) without prior written permission of the author, except as provided by United States of America copyright law.

All material contained herein that is not original is reprinted with authorized permission or license from the authors, artists, and/or publishers with appropriate attributions, or are in the public domain, or within the publishers' gratis use guidelines.

Scriptures marked RSV are taken from the REVISED STANDARD VERSION®, Grand Rapids: Copyright© 1971, Used by permission of Zondervan.

Scriptures marked NIV are taken from the THE HOLY BIBLE, NEW INTERNATIONAL VERSION®. Copyright© 1973, 1978, 1984, 2011 by Biblica, Inc.TM. Used by permission of Zondervan.

Library of Congress Catalog Number: 2021951901
Disraeli, Stephen, Author
The Unseen Husband, by Stephen Disraeli
Advantage Books, Longwood, FL, 2022
ISBN (print): 9781597556743
    (ePub):9781597556828

First Printing: March 2022
21 22 23 24 25 26 27   10 9 8 7 6 5 4 3 2 1

Table of Contents

FOREWORD 7

1: DRAW ME AFTER YOU (SONG OF SOLOMON CHAPTER 1) 9

2: ARISE MY LOVE, MY FAIR ONE (SONG OF SOLOMON CHAPTER 2) 15

3: I WILL SEEK HIM (SONG OF SOLOMON CHAPTER 3)..21

4: MY SISTER, MY BRIDE (SONG OF SOLOMON CHAPTER 4).................................25

5: I AM SICK WITH LOVE (SONG OF SOLOMON CHAPTER 5)...................................31

6: THE DANCE OF THE SHULAMMITE (SONG OF SOLOMON CHAPTER 6) 35

7: O QUEENLY MAIDEN (SONG OF SOLOMON CHAPTER 7) 39

8: MAKE HASTE, MY BELOVED (SONG OF SOLOMON CHAPTER 8) 43

Stephen Disraeli

Foreword

The Song of Solomon is a love-dialogue between a distressed wife, grieving over an apparently lost husband, and the faithful, persevering husband himself.

Christian understanding of this book has been affected by fashions in the reading of the Bible. The church of the Middle Ages was content to find allegory in any part of scripture. In this case, the classic interpreter is Bernard of Clairvaux, who explains "black but beautiful" as a description of the Christian church and of the Christian soul, sin-stained but redeemed. Protestantism reacted against the over-use of allegory by insisting on a return to more strictly literal interpretations of scripture. Unfortunately this may lead us into rejecting allegory even when the writer cannot have intended anything else. I have heard people call the Song of Solomon a "merely human" love-story. I have heard them suggest that the book does not rightly belong in a religious canon at all.

We need to remind ourselves why the Old Testament came together. Nobody was intending to make a collection of "Hebrew literature". Every genre that we find there has been adapted for the purpose of saying something about Israel's God. We find origin legends, law, history, collections of proverbs. None of these books come without a message of some kind about the nature of God. Why would the Song of Solomon be an exception?

In fact the Song is not an exception. It belongs to the genre of "love poetry" to the same extent that Kings and Chronicles belong to the genre of "history", or Proverbs belongs to the genre "collection of proverbs and wise sayings". In each case the literary genre has been given a spiritual dimension. It is easy to see that the "historical" books are not just pure secular history, but have been used to say something about the relation between God and his people. The same can be said for the collections of law. We find in Proverbs not just secular wisdom, but warnings against different kinds of unrighteousness. Similarly the writer of the Song of Solomon has taken the genre of "love-poetry" and adapted it to the well-established prophetic theme of the marriage relationship between God and his people Israel.

Specifically, it is a more encouraging and optimistic version of the wrathful allegories of Ezekiel ch16, and ch23, touching on Israel's faults but focussing on the promise of restoration. Like Ezekiel's allegory, the Song of Solomon is a response to the catastrophe of the Babylonian conquest of Jerusalem, and the state of exile which followed.

The first part of the book dwells on the blissful relationship of the past, in the ideal state symbolised by nostalgic memories of Solomon's kingdom. This idyll is interrupted by the devastating scene in which the wife "loses" her husband, reflecting the fears of exiled Israel about the end of the special relationship.

The rest of the book is occupied by two parallel themes. On the one hand, the wife yearning for her "absent" husband. On the other hand, that same husband pouring out reassurances about his continuing love and continuing presence by her side. His task is made more difficult because, of course, she cannot see him. She will not be convinced until she learns, once more, how to recognise his voice.

I hope to be able to demonstrate that this approach to the Song of Solomon offers a more complete explanation of the book than can be found in more secular interpretations. I won't be reading this book in a devotional way, but I would argue that gaining a good sense of the writer's conscious intentions provides the most sure foundation of any approach, including the devotional.

A note on terminology. The couple in this poem are frequently labelled as "Lover" and "Beloved". Since they both love each other with equal force, the names are ambiguous. I shall avoid the ambiguity by calling them "Girl" and "Husband".

Quotations in this discussion will normally come from the Revised Standard Version (RSV). The New International Version (NIV) is also mentioned. Since I am not an American, the famous translation published in 1611 will be identified as the Authorised Version (AV).

1

Draw Me After You

(Song of Solomon Chapter 1)

V1 "The Song of Songs, which is Solomon's."
My theory of the context of Song of Solomon won't allow the assumption that this book was written by Solomon himself, or even during Solomon's lifetime. At most, the opening statement could only be a form of dedication to Solomon, as the ideal king (in nostalgic memory) of Israel's ideal kingdom. His name is derived from the word for "peace", which sums up and defines what Israel is looking for.

V2 "O that you would kiss me with the kisses of your mouth."
This verse sets the tone for the whole poem, which begins (as it ends) with a speech from the Girl.
Telling her Husband that she wants his love, she compares him with the pleasant taste of wine and the pleasant smell of oil, and his name with the gentle touch of oil.

V3 "Therefore the maidens love you."
Who are these maidens? If Israel's God is also the Creator God, then he has a relationship of some kind with all the nations of the world, even if they are not conscious of the fact.

V4 "Draw me after you, let us make haste."
The Girl may be expressing her desire to follow him, admitting that she needs his help to do so. Alternatively, she now speaks to the maidens mentioned in the previous verse, proposing that all of them should pursue the Husband together. At the same time, she stakes her claim to a "special relationship"; "The king has brought me into his chambers."

"We will exult and rejoice in you; we will extol your love more than wine".

Addressing the Husband again, the Girl says "We" because she now speaks for that whole band of maidens, not just for herself. "Rightly do they love you."

V5 "I am very dark, but comely, O daughters of Jerusalem."

She is dark like the tents of Kedar (an alien tribe) and comely like the curtains of Solomon. The message is that both statements are true at the same time. Her imperfections are not an obstacle to her Husband's love.

V6 "Do not gaze upon me because the sun has scorched me."

She is a poor peasant girl, marked as such by the acquired tan of her outdoor occupations. She expects to face the social scorn of the urban girls, especially the high-class maidens in their sun-sheltered chambers. Israel in exile was very conscious of her low social status among the great nations of the world. So if Israel is the peasant girl, the other nations of the world themselves must be the "daughters of Jerusalem" addressed in these verses.

"My mother's sons made me keeper of the vineyards."

Why not "the sons of my father"? I think the simplest answer is "polygamy". If a man could have more than one wife, the children of the same mother would be a distinct and more compact group, a very strong social support. When Tamar was raped by her half-brother Amnon, it was her full brother Absalom who took her under his wing (2 Samuel ch.13). It seems that a girl's most natural protectors and guardians, in that kind of society, would be the sons of her own mother, closer sometimes even than her father.

It's evident that she comes from a local family and works under the authority of her immediate relatives. This rules out one suggestion, prompted by the word "black", that she was a slave. Slavery in the ancient world was not associated with skin colour.

1: Draw Me After You

"My mother' sons were angry with me, they made me keeper of the vineyards; but my own vineyard I have not kept."

Her brothers are God's agents in placing Israel within the world. In that capacity, they have given her responsibility of some sort for the vineyards of the world in general. Yet she has made a bad start, by neglecting even her own personal vineyard (an allusion to the parable about Israel's faults in Isaiah ch5). Their anger is the end-result of that sequence, not the starting-point.

V7 "Tell me where you pasture your flock, where you make it lie down at noon."

In a change of occupation or metaphor, the Girl is now tending a flock of young goats. Of course the same attitude of protective watchfulness is needed in both tasks. Her difficulty in following her Husband is that she cannot trace his movements. She lives a seemingly detached life in the middle of nations with more visible gods ("your companions"). It's like having a secret marriage.

V8 "Follow in the tracks of the flock and pasture your kids beside the shepherds' tents."

His answer is that if she doesn't know where to find him, she should attach herself to those who do ("the shepherds") and follow their guidance.

In many translations, this verse is given to the "Friends", or whatever they're calling their third-party chorus. I'm not sure why. Since the question was addressed to the Husband, it does make sense to assume that the Husband himself is responding to it. Given that assumption, though, there's a paradox at the heart of this exchange. How can this couple be in contact with each other, if the whole point of her question is that they are out of touch?

The answer is that the relationship is asymmetrical- he can see her, though she can't see him. This would not work in a human love-story, which may be why translators refuse to entertain it, but it's a natural description of the relationship between Israel and her God.

11

V9 "I compare you, my love, to a mare of Pharaoh's chariots."

Pharaoh could be expected to have beautiful horses, perhaps ornamented as in the next verse, and of course the Girl is equally attractive.

V11 "We will make you ornaments of gold."

He offers to supplement her ornaments with others. He says "We", because he's not a goldsmith or a jeweller and he's not going to make them with his own hands. He's going to give the commission to his servants, who will instruct the craftsmen. We are already returning to the image of "the king", first used in v4.

V12 "My nard gave forth its fragrance."

The next three verses are the Girl's response to his compliments. She is hardly in a position to describe his appearance in detail, so she enjoys his fragrance. She finds him as fragrant as the bag of herbs that lies between her breasts, or the henna that can be found in the vineyards of Engedi. Fragrance comes from her own herbs- her nard- drawn out by the king's presence on his couch.

V15 "Behold, you are beautiful… your eyes are doves."

This exclamation comes from the Husband (the Girl echoes it in the next verse). Both characters use the "dove" comparison later in the book, but the Husband says "your eyes" again (ch4 v1) and the Girl says "his eyes" (ch5 v12). That's another symptom of the asymmetrical relationship. The Husband will normally address the Girl directly, but she tends to talk about him to other people.

Vv16-17 "Our couch is green; the beams of our house are cedar, our rafters are pine."

Some people see a reference here to the wooden panelling of the Temple of Solomon. Given the green couch, I would take the picture the other way round. I believe the trees are literal, and the house structure is metaphorical. In other words, the "chambers" in which the king lives (v4) are the open spaces of the land.

This chapter has introduced the Husband in two different roles, as shepherd and as king. He promises to be "the shepherd of my people" in Ezekiel ch4 v15, and his role as king is familiar from the Psalms and elsewhere.

Readers looking for a merely human love-story in the Song sometimes try to separate them as two characters, creating a rather artificial "love-triangle". There is no evidence for such a drama in the rest of the book. We see no sign of conscious rivalry between two males, no sign that the Girl is faced with a choice, and no sign that she feels moved to reject anyone's love. Since I have my doubts about the later instances of "feeds his flock", the shepherd himself does not appear with any certainty after the single reference in v7. As the supposed preferred lover, he really ought to be more prominent.

Meanwhile it is clear from every speech in this chapter that the Girl loves both characters fervently. So the only way to save her reputation as an honest woman is to identify them, as one and the same.

If we want to find any coherent story in the Song of Solomon, we need to raise our sights above the horizons of human romance.

Stephen Disraeli

2

Arise My Love, My Fair One

(Song of Solomon Chapter 2)

V1 "I am a rose of Sharon, a lily of the valleys."
Here is a continuation of the love-scene which ended the previous chapter. This declaration will encourage us to find allusions to the Girl in later examples of "lilies".

Sharon is a plain on the Mediterranean coast, and therefore on the western side of the land. In the previous chapter, we had a reference to En-gedi, at the southern extremity. The other two points of the compass (Gilead and Lebanon) will be found in a later chapter. So all these geographical references, taken together, will mark out the boundaries of that greater realm of Israel which was attributed to David and Solomon.

V2 "As a lily among brambles, so is my love among maidens."
Meaning, of course, that she stands out against other women in the same way.

V3 "As an apple tree among the trees of the wood, so is my beloved among young men."
We are still in the woodland scene. The point seems to be that the apple tree is almost unique in combining size ("I sat in his shadow") with sweetness of fruit.

V4 "He brought me to the banqueting house."
The "banqueting house" or "house of vines" would be the Loved One's vineyard. So when the Girl speaks of being sustained with the sweetness of raisins and apples, we can imagine them as coming from the vines and the trees which are surrounding the couple.

"His banner over me was love."

She trusts in his protection. An army's banner is announcing the presence of a protecting force.

V6 "O that his left hand were under my head, and that his right hand embraced me."

The Hebrew simply says "His left hand under my head, his right hand embracing me". The RSV and other translators have decided to make this a wish for the future, but the verse fits better into the context if the description is part of the present love-scene.

V7 "I adjure you by the gazelles or the hinds of the field."

The phrase "I adjure by…", like the phrase "I swear by…", should be followed by the name of a deity. They're both appeals to spiritual authority, in support of the statement or request being made. In effect the phrase "gazelles and hinds" has been substituted for the name of God in that sentence. This may be because of the understanding of Israel's God as a Living God, providing the Life which fills the creatures and inspires their motion. But since the Girl is on the verge of spending the next half-chapter describing her lover as a gazelle, this phrase comes close to confirming that her lover is God himself.

The term "daughters of Jerusalem" was introduced in the first chapter for the social superiors of the peasant girl, scorning her low status. That is, in terms of the basic allegory, the other nations of the world, who are rivals for the Husband's love.

"That you stir up nor awaken love until it please."

At least one translation gives the injunction as "Do not wake my beloved until she pleases", which suggests a romantic picture of sleeping maiden and watchful, protective male. The problem is that this verse is clearly part of the continuing speech of the Girl. She addresses the daughters of Jerusalem on half a dozen other occasions, while her Husband never does, Two of those occasions (ch3 v5, ch8 v4) are

2: Arise My Love, My Fair One

repetitions of this very verse, and in the latter case this verse and the previous verse are repeated as a unit. It is part of her speech pattern.

The AV offers "till he please", which fits the scene better but gets the gender of the verb wrong. The implication of the RSV translation is that her state of love is enjoying a nostalgic dream of rest and mutual enjoyment, from which she does not want to be awoken. If this book is written after the great catastrophe of Jerusalem, then every allusion to the old idyllic relationship is retrospective.

V8 "The voice of my beloved! Behold he comes."

There is now a change of scene. The premise of the new scene is that the Girl is keeping herself indoors, remaining at home in seclusion. She sees him as a sleek gazelle, leaping around the mountains. Even in his role as a gazelle, he behaves like any anxious human suitor, standing on the other side of the walls that keep him away from the woman he loves, trying to gain a sight of her.

V9 "My beloved speaks and says to me…"

We are still wrapped up in the Girl's experience (her dream?), so we don't hear the words of the gazelle in his own voice. We hear him in the Girl's voice, reporting what she's heard him say.

V10 "Arise, my love, my fair one, and come away."

The gazelle's appeal is a self-contained poem, beginning and ending with these words. He invites her to leave her house and join him in the countryside, now that the winter is over and the land is coming back to life. The early rains have done their work and gone away. The flowers can be seen. The song of the turtle-dove and the other birds can be heard. The fragrance of the vines can be smelt. The figs on the fig-trees are ready to be tasted. So she can revel in the landscape using a full range of senses (touch was catered for in the earlier scene). Come out, my love, and share in the enjoyment of all these things.

V14 "My dove, in the clefts of the rock…"

17

The same kind of invitation, with a different image. Now she's one of the wild doves which nest in the crevices of the rock-face. He calls her to come out of this protective home, so that he can see her beautiful face and hear her sweet voice.

V15 "Catch us the foxes."
But the enjoyment of the spring landscape is not just about passive observation. There is work to be done. The vines are in blossom and need to be protected against intruders. This is the task which she had been neglecting in the first chapter.

V16 "My beloved is mine and I am his, he pastures his flock among the lilies."
This, too, is part of her speech pattern, and we will see it again. The words "his flock" are not found in the Hebrew, which just says "feeds". The addition is misleading, because this is not a one-verse return to the image of the shepherd. Gazelles "feed among the lilies" (ch4 v5), and that must be what is happening here. Since the Girl has already identified herself as a lily, the implication is that the Husband "feeds" on close contact with the Girl (and those like her).

V17 "Until the day breathes and the shadows flee."
The action of this verse will last all day until the dusk, when the sunset breeze arrives and the shadows lengthen. If it meant "until dawn", then the gazelle would be running about all night, which would not be convenient.

V18 "Turn, my beloved, be like a gazelle, or like a young stag upon rugged mountains."
I suggest that "turn" is describing the repeated action of turning, running backwards and forwards, and round and round, in joyful exuberance. When the gazelle was appealing to the woman, he was celebrating the arrival of new life in the land, and this looks like a physical expression of the same thing, another aspect of the sensory enjoyment.

2: Arise My Love, My Fair One

So the first part of this chapter was about the mutual enjoyment of Girl and Husband, and the second part has been about their shared enjoyment of the world which the Husband has created.

Stephen Disraeli

3

I Will Seek Him

(Song of Solomon Chapter 3)

V1 "Upon my bed at night I sought him whom my soul loves… I sought him but found him not."

Here is the Girl's response to the gazelle's invitation in the previous chapter. The word "soul" has been compromised, for modern readers, by the mediaeval concept of the detachable soul, so it may be misleading in translations of scripture. In fact she loves him with her NEPHESH. The very life that is in her is in love with her Husband and wants to seek him out. Very natural, indeed, if the Husband is also the source of the life that is in her.

V2 "I will rise now and go about the city… I sought him and found him not."

She could not find him on her bed, so she goes out into the streets. This does not necessarily clash with the "peasant girl" picture, because her vineyard and pasture could be just outside the city walls,

V3 "The watchmen found me… Scarcely had I passed them when I found him who my soul loves."

This first encounter with the watchmen was evidently enough to make the difference in her search. It would seem that seeking their help was the right thing to do. A dramatized version of the Song ought to show them pointing her in the right direction.

V4 "I would not let him go until I had brought him into my mother's house, and into the chamber of her that conceived me."

The choice of her mother's chamber may be practical, and it may be symbolic. As a practical issue, a large family without much wealth could hardly afford the luxury of a separate chamber for each child. Her mother's chamber might be the only place where she could get any privacy.

At the same time, it shows that the relationship is not a clandestine relationship. The clear implication is that it has her mother's approval. That's a reason for considering the symbolic function of the Girl's mother, who is quite an important background figure in this poem. The label "her that conceived me" is not just the normal repetition of Hebrew poetry. It points to the fact that the mother is the most immediate source of the same NEPHESH that has been yearning to find her Husband. If the Girl represents Israel, then her mother would represent the historic roots of Israel. Following on from this, her mother's chamber could be identified as the land in which Israel has established a marriage relationship.

V5 Since the rendezvous in her mother's chamber creates another love-scene, following the woodland scene of the previous chapter, the Girl repeats the request she made in ch2 v7.

V6 "What is that coming up from the wilderness, like a column of smoke, perfumed with myrrh and frankincense?"

The answer to this question must be found in Israel's history. The wilderness is the unsettled territory beyond Israel's borders, on the far side of the Jordan. Israel's God led Israel through the wilderness in the form of a column of smoke. Myrrh and frankincense are among the ingredients of the sacred oil and incense described in Exodus ch30, so they may be associated with this column. Israel and her God (represented by the Ark) then entered the land together. In history, then, it is Israel's God that "comes up from the wilderness". The new arrival is in the feminine gender (compare ch8 v5), but in this case that would also fit the column itself.

V7 "Behold, it is the litter of Solomon!"

Our reading of this announcement needs to be controlled by our understanding of the previous verse. This is not the historic Solomon, but

3: I Will Seek Him

Solomon "man of peace", ideal king of the ideal kingdom, the symbolic representative of the God of Israel.

For one thing, a wedding procession of the historic Solomon would not have begun that far out. The word "wilderness" does not include the near vicinity of Jerusalem.

"About it are sixty mighty men."

As befits a king, especially a divine king, Solomon is accompanied by Power. David had a band of thirty mighty men (1 Chronicles ch.11), and Solomon's bodyguard is twice as large. Evidently "one greater than David" is here.

V9 "King Solomon made himself a palanquin from the wood of Lebanon":

As befits a king, especially a divine king, Solomon is accompanied by Glory. He arrives in comfort and luxury, carried in a litter. When God and his people entered the land from the wilderness, the Ark was carried across the Jordan like a litter, accompanied by the Tent of Meeting. This combination is the lineal ancestor of Solomon's Temple, which was built with the wood of Lebanon and gloriously decorated with gold and silver and purple, just like the litter described here. These decorations are lovingly made by the daughters of Jerusalem.

V11 "Behold king Solomon, with the crown with which his mother crowned him on the day of his wedding."

The summons is addressed to the "daughters of Zion". They must be representing the true people of God, so they need to be distinguished from what the Song has been calling "daughters of Jerusalem".

Some people believe that the purpose of the Song of Songs was to celebrate the wedding of the historic King Solomon. So I'm tempted to ask- "Which one?" Solomon is credited with seven hundred wives, and it's not likely that any of these marriages was a love-match. But if Solomon represents the God of Israel, then "the wedding of Solomon" represents the act which unites God with his people, making them husband and wife.

Evidently the wedding took place previously, since he is wearing the wedding crown already. Then what do we make of the crowning of the bridegroom by his mother, a very obscure part of the ceremonial? I think the key to understanding this event is to remember the name of Solomon's mother, Bathsheba. That is, "daughter of the oath". So the significance of the act is that God's marriage with his people has been sealed by his solemn oath, which we know as the oath of the Covenant.

Then the symbolism of this passage points to the arrival in the land of a God and his people, already bound in a solemn covenant relationship.

4

My Sister, My Bride

(Song of Solomon Chapter 4)

V1 "Behold, you are beautiful, my love… Your eyes are doves behind your veil."

The king was introduced as a bridegroom in the previous chapter, and the present chapter is occupied by the praise of his bride. He begins by repeating his words from ch1 v15. Like doves, perhaps, because of their whiteness (though I'm aware that doves can come in different colours).

The fact that she wears a veil shows her to be a bride, or at least a married woman. The custom is illustrated in the story of Isaac and Rebekah. The first time that Rebekah sees Isaac, she covers herself with her veil (Genesis ch24 vv64-5). This is not because she wants to hide her face from Isaac himself, but because she regards herself as his wife, from that moment onwards. As an unmarried girl, of course, she had left her face visible for all to see.

"Your hair is like a flock of goats, moving down the slopes of Gilead."

This comparison may be about the picture seen from a distance, the colour flowing down against the lighter background.

I can also see this line as an example of what I call the "equal excellence" comparison. That is to say, the Girl's hair is excellent, as hair, to the same degree that a flock of goats is excellent as a flock of goats. Not necessarily in the same way. To the owner of the goats, the sight of the flock would be a welcome sign of wealth. Gilead, on the eastern side of the Jordan, would be good pasture ground, so the goats would be well-fed and profitable.

From personal experience (see Dedication), I would advise against offering this passage as an intended compliment. This line is one of those details which could be taken in the wrong way. Though the hair on a prize goat might, perhaps, be sleek and well-combed (rather than "lank and straggly").

V2 "Your teeth are like a flock of shorn ewes that have come up from the washing, all of which bear twins, and not one of them is bereaved."

The first line appears to be about visible whiteness. The second line is normally taken as the rather unromantic compliment "None of your teeth are missing", though this would work better if the wording was "All of them ARE twins".

Once again, I'd like to offer an alternative explanation in terms of the flock as a source of wealth. The best kind of sheep is the fertile sheep, because the owner sees the lambs or the promise of lambs. If all the ewes are bearing twins, and there aren't any miscarriages, then the expected increase of wealth would be enormous. So the Girl's teeth are excellent to the same degree that a fast-breeding flock of sheep is excellent.

V3 "Your lips are like scarlet thread… Your cheeks are like halves of a pomegranate."

These are straightforward comparisons of appearance. Translators hesitate between "cheeks" and "forehead". I would stay with "cheeks", because the gaze is clearly travelling downwards.

V4 "Your neck is like a tower of David… whereupon hang a thousand bucklers"

This may be because the tower of David is tall, with a smooth surface, built with strength and grace. Edith Swan-neck, the wife of King Harold of England, was another woman famed for the same feature. Perhaps it is the ornaments around the Girl's neck that remind him the shields (of defeated warriors?) which hang on the walls of the tower.

V5 "Your two breasts are like two fawns, twins of a gazelle."

That is, they move with grace and delicacy. This allusion to gazelles prompts the writer to repeat, almost automatically, what was said about the original gazelle on a previous occasion (ch2 vv16-17), all the way from "feeding among the lilies" to "the shadows flee."

V6 "I will hie me to the mountain of myrrh and the hill of frankincense."

Then this declaration is the equivalent of the next words in that chapter, about the gazelle turning upon the mountains. At the same time, there is an allusion to the "column of smoke", perfumed with myrrh and frankincense, which represents the divine king's first arrival in the land (ch3 v6). He expects to find the same pleasure in his people that he finds in the land itself.

V7 "Come with me from Lebanon, my bride… Depart from the peak of Amarna, from the peak of Senir and Hermon."

A common understanding of this invitation is that he's calling her away from a dangerous region, "the haunt of lions and leopards". But that conflicts with the valuation of Lebanon which we find in the rest of the poem, as the source of good things, fine woods and sweet perfumes, and there was no previous suggestion that she was getting into a place of danger.

In fact the Lebanon is not an alien land, but part of the territory of the ideal kingdom. The expression "Depart from…" can also be translated as "Look down from…" In other words, he's not really calling her to leave the mountain area at all.

On the contrary, the invitation is that they should wander together from one range to another, enjoying the mountain area like the gazelle at the end of the second chapter. In which case the point of mentioning lions and leopards would be that these are living things, beautiful things, which enjoy the use of the same country. Their presence is to be celebrated, not feared. They are as much part of the Life of the land as the living things praised in the second chapter- the gazelle and the stag, the turtledove, the flower, the fig, and the vine.

I've already remarked on the significance of the geographical references. In the first chapter, there was En-gedi, in the extreme south. The next chapter mentioned the Plain of Sharon, in the west. This passage has brought in Gilead, in the east, and Lebanon, to the north. All these references, taken together, mark out the boundaries of that greater kingdom of Israel which was attributed to David and Solomon. In this passage, the Husband is expressing his love for the Girl, and also inviting her, as in the second chapter, to a shared enjoyment of his Creation.

V9 "You have ravished my heart, my sister, my bride".

A fresh poem of praise begins at this point. This is where he begins calling her a sister, so modern readers are puzzled, and modern scholars get excited enough to start talking about the marriage practices of the Egyptian Pharaohs.

Yet I don't know that "my sister, my bride" is an odder combination than "Turn, O backsliding children, saith the Lord, for I am married to you", which is the AV translation of Jeremiah ch3 v14. The names of Israelites in the Old Testament show that people could see their God in a number of different relations- "My father", "My brother", "My friend". All these relations, if they are between God and his people, are metaphorical, and can be combined to provide a fuller picture.

Only those who persist in seeing the Song as a sentimental human romance need have any problem with the phrase.

The first part of the chapter was focussed on the Girl's appearance. The second poem is more about the effect she has on him. He says she has stolen his heart, taken control of his love. A single glance of her eyes, or a single flash of her jewellery, was enough to do the job.

V10 "How sweet is your love."

The remarks about "better than wine" and the fragrance of her oils are an echo of what the Girl herself said about him in the opening verses. He praises the sweetness of her lips and tongue and compares the fragrance of her garments with the scent of Lebanon.

V12 "A garden locked, a fountain sealed."

These are two distinct comparisons, with similar meanings. In both respects, she is a source of life As a garden, she is producing an abundance of sweet-tasting and sweet-smelling fruits and spices, including the significant frankincense. As a fountain, she is providing a well of living water. In addition, she has the flowing streams from Lebanon (one of the references treating Lebanon as a source of good things).

In both respects, at the same time, the Woman is enclosed and sealed. As bride of the Husband, she belongs to the Husband and to nobody else.

V16 "Let my beloved come to his garden."

This verse interrupts the poem of praise. Since the Girl is being compared with a garden, she responds to the comparison by inviting her Husband to come and join her there. She calls upon the winds to spread the scent of it far and wide, so that he might be tempted by the scents and come to enjoy the fruits.

Stephen Disraeli

5

I Am Sick With Love

(Song of Solomon Chapter 5)

V1 "I come to my garden."
The chapter division is clearly in the wrong place. This verse is the climax of the previous chapter. It is a declaration of intent, on the Husband's part, prompted by his contemplation of the bride. In the present arrangement of the Song, it's also a response to the Girl's invitation in the last verse of that chapter. He comes to enjoy all the sweet things which the garden offers, the myrrh and the honey, the wine and the milk. His ownership of the garden is emphasised by the nine-fold repetition of "my". The Girl can only offer her Husband what already belongs to him.

The second part of the verse is an exchange very appropriate for a wedding feast;

Groom and Bride to Guests; "Eat, O friends, and drink".

Guests to Groom and Bride; "Drink deeply, O lovers".

That's the natural conclusion of the first portion of the Song, which has been celebrating the relation of Girl and Husband as a loving couple.

The passage that follows is the central episode of the Song of Solomon, because it explains why the poem was written.

V2 "I slept, but my heart was awake."
Once again, the Girl is at home in bed. Her mind may be asleep, but her heart is awake, and therefore sensitive to the approach of her Husband. He knocks on the door and calls on her (still calling her his sister and his dove) to let him in. He complains that his head is wet with the dews of night.

v3 "I had put off my garment, how could I put it on?"

However, the Girl is slow to respond. Getting up to answer the door would also involve getting her feet dirty again (which may say something about the poverty of the implied household).

Vv4 -5 "My beloved put his hand to the latch, and my heart was thrilled within me… my hands dripped with myrrh."

Commentators find erotic overtones in these verses. But the Girl's next action, in moving to the household door, is such a vital part of the overall picture that the more natural meaning of "latch" needs to be taken at face-value. The presence of myrrh is one of the signs that her Husband has been there, at least.

V6 "I opened to my beloved".

Yet when the door is opened, she finds a paradox. The impatient Husband cannot be seen. She goes looking for him, as she did before, but she cannot find him, and he doesn't answer her calling. Once again, "I sought him and found him not". His mysterious disappearance and her fruitless pursuit are turning the story into something like a dream, or rather a nightmare.

v7 "The watchmen found me… they wounded me, they took away my mantle."

The climax of the nightmare is her second encounter with the watchmen. On this occasion, they have clearly turned against her. We might have a better understanding of this episode if we knew the significance of the confiscated clothing. One common interpretation of the scene, taking "city watchmen" literally, is that they identified her as a harlot. That could explain the beating, of course, but why would that be a reason to remove one of her garments? Is that a normal police response to street prostitution?

We need to account for the change in their attitude between the two encounters. In an earlier version of this explanation, I took the watchmen as a representation of secular authority. However, an old friend of mine (see Dedication) observed, with unnecessary diffidence, that she would otherwise have thought them to be the prophets. She was right, of course. As I should have realised more quickly, these figures are borrowed directly from Ezekiel's "watchman" metaphor (Ezekiel ch33). They are removing some garment which identifies her as a married woman, because, as prophets, they are questioning her married status.

This whole episode of "waking and search" is the key to understanding the Song of Solomon. It's a description, in allegory, of the psychological impact of that great catastrophe, the Fall of Jerusalem and the captivity in Babylon. Israel feels a sense of loss, a sense of separation from her God. There is also a sense that her neglect of his persistent call is part of the reason for the separation In the better days of the relationship, the function of the prophets was to point her in his direction. In the aftermath of disaster, some of the prophets are giving her a verbal beating, declaring that the covenant has been broken and that her precious marriage has been dissolved. The purpose of the Song of Solomon is to present the more positive message (also found in Jeremiah and Ezekiel) that the relationship will be restored.

The second half of the Song is an asymmetrical dialogue involving (not quite "between") the Girl and her Husband. She spends her time telling other people about him and grieving his absence. He spends his time addressing her directly, as a promise of his continued presence.

V8 " I adjure you, O daughters of Jerusalem, if you find my husband, tell him I am sick with love."

That is, she wants him to return. "Sick with love" was also used in the happier circumstances of ch2 v5.

V9 "What is your beloved more than another beloved?"

This is the first of two questions which serve as connecting links, introducing further declarations from the Girl. I've suggested that the "daughters of Jerusalem" are the other nations of the world, socially superior to Israel (in their own minds) in the same way that city girls are superior to peasants. Naturally they cannot see that the Husband attached to the people of Israel is unique, or any better than his "companions" (ch1 v7), the other gods known by the world.

V10 "My husband is all radiant and ruddy, distinguished among ten thousand."

This opens a description which is the counterpart of his own description of the Girl, in the fourth chapter. One similarity is that the survey begins at the head and works downwards. One difference is that she says "he is" rather than "you are". She has no consciousness of being in his presence.

The first point is the overall radiance of his figure. There is praise by contrast; he is unique among ten thousand, presumably as a red-blooded warrior. If his hair is black, it must be his face that is golden.

His eyes can be compared, for whiteness, with doves and milk. Once again, there is a reference to myrrh, one of the spices which accompanied the divine "column of smoke" (ch3 v6).

V14 "His arms are rounded gold, set with jewels. His body is ivory work, encrusted with sapphires."

Commentators have suggested that the overall description was inspired by a statue. The resemblance is most obvious in these verses, covering the body below the head. It could be another example of "equal excellence"; the Husband has all the qualities desirable for his own person, in the same way that such a statue has all the qualities desirable for an ideal statue. But there is also an implied contrast, in that he is a living figure, while the similar statues of all the other gods are completely lifeless.

v16 "His speech is most sweet."

His voice, indeed, could not be the voice of a statue. As Isaiah observes, the statues of the gods are unable to speak. The voice is left to be the climax of the description, as the feature which she values most. This is not just about the sweetness of the sound, but about the content of his words. What he says is more important than anything in his looks. That's another reason to identify him as the God of Israel, who makes himself known in the way that he speaks to his people.

6

The Dance of the Shulammite

(Song of Solomon Chapter 6)

V1 "Whither has your beloved gone?"
This is the second "connecting link" question, introducing a further statement from the Girl.

V2 "My beloved has gone down to his garden to the beds of spices."
Strictly speaking, she could not have given this information, because the whole point of her appeal is that she does not know where he is. However, the answer given is not as specific as it appears. It amounts to saying that he is enjoying his Creation. The key to finding him and resuming contact may be that she needs to go and do the same thing.

The second part of v2 combines and links this "garden" theme with the "feeding among the lilies" theme of the next verse. V3 is a repetition of the refrain in ch2 v16 (and the RSV repeats the mistranslation "pastures his flock"). Then the Husband begins a fresh poem of praise for the Girl.

V4 "You are as beautiful as Tirzah, my love, comely as Jerusalem."
This is a remarkable combination, because these were the two capitals (before the building of Samaria) of the two kingdoms into which Solomon's realm divided. Naming them both together offers a kind of forgiveness for the schism- though the writer is not quite forgiving enough to name Samaria. It's like the attempt in Zechariah ch11 to re-forge the bond of union between the two nations (who were destined, however, to remain separate as "the Jews" and "the Samaritans").

We may be startled, at first, by the praise of the Girl as "terrible as an army with banners". But we in modern times may call a woman "stunning" or "drop-dead gorgeous", which carry a similar thought. That is, the man is overwhelmed by the woman's beauty, unable to stand in her presence. For the same reason he asks her to turn her eyes away from him, to reduce their impact.

The remainder of v5 and the two following verses are taken from the praise which followed the praise of her eyes in the fourth chapter.

V8 "There are sixty queens and eighty concubines."

It isn't easy to account for these estimates. The historic King Solomon had many more of both .The explanation "This was the number he had at the time of writing" will not do, in my understanding of the context of the Song. The exact numbers are less important than the fact that they are large numbers.

V9 "My dove is only one, the darling of her mother."

In contrast with the above, the Girl is unique, true to her roots and singled out as a bride.

One possible explanation of the crowd of women would be that the queens, concubines and maidens are the different kinds of states and ethnic groups found in the world. These also belong to the Husband, of course, but they have not been singled out in the same way. That is why they call her "happy".

V10 "Who is this that looks forth like the dawn, fair as the moon, bright as the sun?"

It may be best to take this as part of the praise given by the other ladies.

V11 "I went down to the nut orchard".

We return for the moment to the Girl's voice. She is checking the progress of the blossoms and vines and pomegranates, perhaps in advance of the invitation which will be offered in the next chapter.

V12 "My fancy set me in a chariot beside my prince."

Everybody agrees on the difficulty of rendering this verse. The literal translation is that the NEPHESH, or "life" of the speaker, taking her unawares, put her in some relation with a chariot- either "like it" or "in it".

6: The Dance of the Shulammite

To be "like a chariot" would imply speed, maybe in the sense that her thoughts were "taking wing". As for the driver of the chariot, we are offered a choice between "my prince" or "prince of my people", and "Amminadib". The only parallel I can offer in the latter case is the Amminadab who appears at the end of Ruth as the ultimate ancestor of the house of David, and thus the ancestor of Solomon.

However, the given translation seems to offer the most reasonable interpretation for the context. The Girl was among the blossoms and vines looking for her Husband, Then her imagination (she thinks) took hold of her and placed her in his presence. She's already there in reality, also, but she doesn't understand that yet.

V13 "Return, O Shulammite."

This name may be related (like "Solomon") to the word for "peace". It only occurs here, though people often apply it over the rest of the poem.

The verse is a dialogue. The onlookers want her to "return"- that is, perhaps, to continue the dancing movement. Her response seems to come from her lack of assurance- "Why should you look at her?"

"... as upon a dance before two armies."

"Two armies" is a translation of Mahanaim, which is also a place-name, and it may be better to leave it as a place-name. This is another allusion to the long-lost territories on the eastern side of the Jordan.

In the story of Jacob's return from exile, he gave this name to the place where he saw a vision of God's heavenly army reinforcing his own host. When David was driven out of Jerusalem by Absolom's rebellion, Mahanaim was the place where he found refuge until Absolom had been defeated. Both stories have something to say about temporary exile, and about the power of God in those circumstances, which may encourage a Girl who feels exiled from her Husband.

The very fact that Mahanaim has an origin-story in Genesis implies that the place was an important cultic centre in ancient Israel. In other words, a place where sacred festivals would have been held. That is enough to explain the reference to dancing, as part of an act of worship. So the message of this dialogue is that the Girl may, if she rallies her courage, regard herself as worshipping God in a place of short-term exile, from which she will return with God's help. This applies, of course, to her literal exile in Babylon, as well as to her metaphorical exile from her Husband's presence.

7

O Queenly Maiden

(Song of Solomon Chapter 7)

V1 "How graceful are your feet in sandals, O queenly maiden."
The Husband now pictures his Girl as a dancer, following on from the image at the end of the last chapter. Naturally, then, he begins this poem of praise at the sight of her dancing feet and works upwards. The suggestion that she is "queenly", the member of a royal family, is in sharp contrast with her own self-image as a poor girl of low status. Sandals are an important detail of luxury, and this may be one of the marks which identify her as a queen.

V2 "Your navel is a rounded bowl that never lacks mixed wine."
Here is another example of what I'm calling "equal excellence". The bowl-shaped navel of this dancing figure is excellent as a navel to the same degree that a bowl unceasingly filled with wine is excellent as a bowl. This comparison is not suitable for teetotallers. The rest of her lower body is appropriately rounded and delicately coloured.

V3 "Your two breasts are like two fawns, twins of a gazelle."
This repeats ch4 v5, though the reference to "lilies" has been transferred to the previous line, made part of the description of the belly.

V4 "Your neck is like an ivory tower."
Like ivory in colour, like a tower in strength and firmness. In ch4,v4, it was "like the tower of David"

"... *pools in Heshbon*
…like a tower of Lebanon, overlooking Damascus.

…crowns you like Carmel."

We find another set of geographical references, echoing the set found in the first chapters. Once again, they are marking out the extent of the old ideal kingdom of Solomon. Her eyes are like pools in Heshbon, part of the long-lost eastern territories then occupied by the Ammonites. Her nose is like a watchtower in the north (in colour?), standing over against hostile Damascus. Finally, the hair that crowns her head reminds him of the forests which crown Mount Carmel in the west. That covers three directions, and the only real landmark in the south has been mentioned once already (En-gedi, ch1 v14)

Vv7-8 "You are stately as a palm-tree, and your beasts are like its clusters. I say I will climb the palm-tree and lay hold of its branches."

The time has come to grasp the nettle and consider the "erotic" aspect of the Song of Songs, which for some people is an obstacle to understanding the poem in a spiritual sense. The poem is undoubtedly sensuous. At different times, it caters for each of the five senses. When it calls the Girl to the enjoyment of the land, it appeals to the sight, the hearing, the taste, and the sense of smell, and the erotic side brings in the sense of touch.

And why not? There is no Biblical objection to a man's eroticism with his own wife, and we need to remember that this couple are man and wife, which makes the time of separation all the more poignant.

I see no reason why the use of sensuous imagery should be a bar to spiritual interpretation. How else should we interpret the diatribes in the sixteenth and twenty-third chapters of Ezekiel ? The language in those passages is so bluntly and brutally sexual that they cannot be read out in church services. They are represented by gaps in the lectionaries. Yet nobody who reads those chapters can have any doubt that they are intended as religious allegory. The Lord, through Ezekiel's mouth, is complaining about the multiple idolatries of the old Israelite kingdoms. His angry condemnations, as the "husband" of these kingdoms, are expressed in the language of sexual jealousy. If all this can be understood as religious allegory, then so can the gentler, more optimistic sensuousness of the Song of Songs.

7: O Queenly Maiden

While we're on the subject of sensuous action, it occurs to me that dance is something of a running theme in the Song of Solomon. The Shulammite is a dancer, and implicitly a dancer in the poem of praise that follows. The running and "returning" of the gazelle among the mountains (ch2 v17) is a kind of celebratory dance, perhaps the original dance which the Shulammite simply echoes in her own way. There's an element of verbal dance in the repetition of passages or set phrases like "feeding among the lilies". In a dramatized version of the Song, a choreographer could have work to do in arranging the movements of Girl and Husband, as a way of expressing the complex relationship between them.

V9 "Your kisses like the best wine that goes down smoothly, gliding over lips and teeth".

There's a puzzle in the wording of this verse. The Hebrew text says "the best wine for my beloved going down", but it seems odd that he should refer to his beloved while he's in the middle of addressing the same person. Some translations simply leave out the word "for my beloved". Others try to cure the anomaly by ending the sentence at "wine", and making the rest a new sentence with a different speaker. For me, this makes things worse, because it means that "going down" is left hanging in limbo, not attached to any subject. Unless they cheat by repeating the word "wine" (NIV), which gives away the fact that a sentence has been broken apart.

The best suggestion I can make is that "for my beloved" is also a phrase which labels a particular quality of wine, reserved for special purposes, in which case his beloved is being compared with wine of that quality.

V10 "I am my beloved's, and his desire is for me."
This was comfortable assurance, in ch2 v16. In the aftermath of the fifth chapter, it has become a declaration of faith.

V11 "Come, my beloved, let us go forth into the fields"
It is a good sign, that she is beginning to address him directly once more. This invitation is the counterpart of the gazelle's invitation, in the second chapter, to share in the enjoyment of the new spring life. It also

takes up his own proposal in ch5 v1. If they find lodging in the fields and villages outside the city, their visit to the vineyards can take place at the earliest possible moment in the day.

V13 "The mandrakes give forth fragrance".

The neglected Leah, mother of Judah and Levi, used her son's mandrakes to purchase a night of love with Jacob, and the result was the birth of Issachar (Genesis ch30 vv14-18). In the same way, perhaps, the Girl hopes that her own love-relationship will be revived and will be fruitful.

"Choice fruits, new as well as old".

She is not just living on the memories of her old relationship, but offering a completely fresh start.

8

Make Haste, My Beloved

(Song of Solomon Chapter 8)

V1 "O that you were like a brother to me."
In the third chapter, the Girl had been able to find her Husband in the streets and bring him home, to her mother's house and chamber. She would like to do that again, and give him spiced wine and the juice of the pomegranate, but now she feels inhibited. She has lost her confidence, after the events of the fifth chapter. But if he really was a brother, born of the same mother, she would be able to seek his company without fearing the disapproval of others. In other words, she longs for a return to the old freedom, when her love could be freely expressed.

Vv3-4 "O that his left hand were under my head…"
These two verses have the same wording as ch2 vv6-7. The difference is in the tone. On the first occasion, they were expressing the comfortable assurance of an established relationship. Now they represent an aspiration, and it's much more appropriate now than it was then to translate them as a wish for the future.

V5 "Who is this coming up from the wilderness, leaning on her beloved?"
This is a similar question to ch2 v6, and it should be getting a similar answer. On the first occasion, it was a column of smoke, perfumed with myrrh and frankincense, representing the God of Israel. So the natural conclusion is that this question points to Israel herself, entering the land from the wilderness and leaning upon her God.

"Under the apple tree I awakened you. There your mother was in travail with you."

The Girl has already (ch2 v3) given "sitting under the apple tree" as an image for living under her Husband's shadow. So this verse implies that she was under his protection even in the circumstances of her birth.

This is a recognisable echo of the Lord God's declaration in Ezekiel ch16 vv4-6. That is, that he had seen the orphan child Jerusalem "on the day that you were born", that he had seen her neglected and "weltering in your blood", and had taken pity on her, telling her to "Live, and grow up like a plant of the field". As I've already observed, I take the view that the allegory in the Song of Solomon is intended as a more benign version of the allegory in Ezekiel.

V6 "Set me as a seal upon your heart."

There is now a short poem on the strength of love, presumably the Girl's love. She would want to be a seal on her Husband's arm, or attached to his chest, so that she should not be separated from him. Love is a fire that is more powerful than death or flood, and is even more powerful than the call of wealth. What place does this poem have in the present context? If the writer's thought is following through Ezekiel's allegory, then the next stage of the story is the "plighting of troth" for the forthcoming marriage (Ezekiel ch16 v8). These words could be suitably attached to that moment.

V8 "We have a little sister."

On the face of it, the speakers are the Girl's brothers, who appeared briefly in the first chapter. When she married, it would presumably be the family's duty to provide a dowry, which might come in the form of ornament. But I think a better approach is to follow through the allegory in Ezekiel. There, the Lord God, in his double capacity as father-figure and prospective husband, provided his bride with elaborate and costly clothing and ornaments in preparation for her marriage to himself (Ezekiel ch16 vv9-13). It seems to me that the same thing is happening here. God

8: Make Haste, My \Beloved

himself is the speaker, in his double capacity as brother-figure (family guardian) and prospective husband.

In Ezekiel, the Lord God waited until "you grew up and became tall and arrived at full maidenhood, and your breasts were formed" (Ezekiel ch16 v7). But these verses tell us that the Girl "has no breasts". She was fully matured in the earlier chapters, so there must be a sense in which she has retrogressed, in her spiritual maturity. She is no longer as ready for the enjoyment of the Covenant relationship as she had been previously. He needs to repeat his protective guidance, so that she can "grow up and become tall".

But when she reaches (once again) a state of readiness for marriage, what should be done? If she was a wall, then "we" would ornament the wall with silver battlements. If she was a door, then the door would be enclosed in fine cedar. No cost would be spared, in short, in giving her a glorious appearance. But since she is neither a wall nor a door, but a bride, the implication is that no cost will be spared in giving her the glorious appearance appropriate for a bride, in preparation for her marriage to himself.

V10 "I was a wall, and my breasts were like towers."

The Girl echoes the previous passage, and adds the claim that she was "in his eyes" (perhaps in the sense of "under his eye") and brought into a state of Peace. This can be equated with the climax of the story in Ezekiel; "Your renown went forth among the nations, because of your beauty, for it was perfect because of the splendour which I had bestowed upon you, says the Lord God" (Ezekiel ch16 v14).

The Hebrew seems to be ambiguous between "I used to be" and "I have become". The first would mean that she was still expressing her regret for the past, when her city and her kingdom and her Peace with her God were still intact. But her Husband's promise about her wedding ornamentation is forward-looking, by definition, and seems to point towards a renewal of her "married" status. This may be an argument for "I have become". The Girl is looking forward with a renewed self-confidence.

V11 "Solomon had a vineyard."

By a natural association of thought, the mention of "peace" brings up the name of Solomon. The Girl sets out the contrast between two vineyards. Solomon's vineyard was leased to "keepers", who each paid him a thousand pieces of silver for the privilege and managed to obtain two hundred for themselves. She holds the other vineyard in her own right, so there is no need for rental agreements. She reproached herself in the first chapter, that she had not "kept" (protected) her vineyard, yet the same vineyard is now a source of pleasure and pride. This begins to look like confidence in restoration. There's even a hint, perhaps, of Jeremiah's promise that the new covenant relationship will be better than the old (Jeremiah ch31 vv31-34).

Vv13-14 "My companions are listening for your voice…
Make haste, my beloved."

The Song closes with the two appeals against the continued state of separation. In the first, the Husband calls the Girl an inhabitant of the gardens, and tells her that he and his companions are longing to hear her speak. This recalls the previous occasions when he's been summoning her; the call of the gazelle in ch2, the invitation to explore the mountains in ch4, the appeal to the dancer at the end of ch6.

In the second appeal, the Girl calls him a gazelle or young stag, and repeats the invitation of ch2 v17, that he should join her on the "mountains of spices". "Make haste, my beloved" is the emotional equivalent of Revelation's "Even so, come Lord Jesus", which makes it a very appropriate conclusion. Thus the Song ends, as it began, with an affirmation of the Girl's love.

I believe I've demonstrated how the proposed interpretation of the Song of Solomon offers at least an effective explanation. It is one of the Biblical responses to the great catastrophe which the community of God's people experienced at the hands of the Babylonians. It expresses their sense of bereavement and isolation from their God. At the same time, the real purpose of the Song is to encourage them to believe in the restoration of the relationship, and to remain faithful.

In other words, those who collected the book among the sacred writings of Israel, believing it to have a spiritual meaning, were correctly grasping the writer's intentions.

What, then, is the spiritual message for the rest of us?

The story of this book is that God's people thought themselves to have lost their God, and they were mistaken. Their grief and sense of desolation was based on a misunderstanding. They had lost sight of him, and they were failing to hear him, but he had not abandoned them. He remained faithful to his promise, continuing to watch over them, which is why the final note of the poem is the prospect of complete reconciliation.

The continuing message, then, is for God's people experiencing similar anxieties at other times. Are they in exile, surrounded by their enemies? Are they, as a community, lost and far from home? Is their sense of sin taking away their sense of the presence of God? Are they, as individuals, lost and far from home? Is their sense of sin, again, taking away their sense of the presence of God?

Under those conditions, they may listen for and hear the voice of their unseen husband, reminding them of his unfailing love.

Stephen Diseaeli. is available for book interviews and personal appearances. For more information email info@advbooks.com

To purchase additional copies of this book, visit our bookstore website: www.advbookstore.com

Longwood, Florida, USA
"we bring dreams to life"™
www.advbookstore.com

www.ingramcontent.com/pod-product-compliance
Lightning Source LLC
Chambersburg PA
CBHW061303040426
42444CB00010B/2491